It's all about …

REMARKABLE RAIN FORESTS

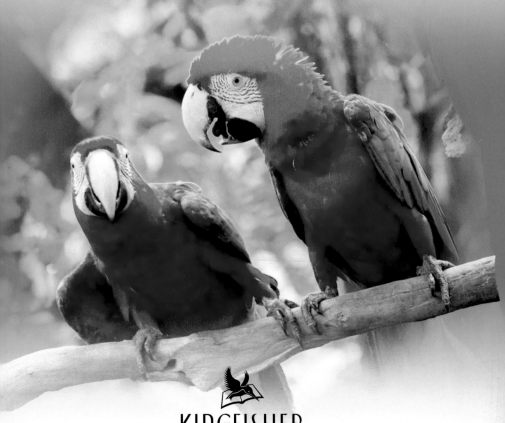

KINGFISHER
NEW YORK

KINGFISHER
LONDON & NEW YORK

Distributed in the U.S. and Canada by Macmillan,
175 Fifth Ave., New York, NY 10010

Library of Congress Cataloging-in-Publication data
has been applied for.

Series editor: Sarah Snashall
Series design: Little Red Ant
Adapted from an original text by James Harrison and Claire Llewellyn

ISBN 978-0-7534-7263-7

Kingfisher books are available for special promotions
and premiums. For details contact: Special Markets
Department, Macmillan, 175 Fifth Ave.,
New York, NY 10010.

For more information, please visit
www.kingfisherbooks.com

Printed in China

9 8 7 6 5 4 3 2 1

1TR/1115/WKT/UG/128MA

Picture credits
The Publisher would like to thank the following for permission to reproduce their material.
Top = t; Bottom = b; Center = c; Left = l; Right = r
Cover Shutterstock/Juriah Mosin; Back cover Shutterstock/cellistka; Pages 4–5b Shutterstock/
szefel; 5 Shutterstock/Sam Chadwick; 6–7 Kingfisher Artbank; 6 Shutterstock/Arangan Ananth;
8–9 Getty/Louise Murray; 8 FLPA/Minden Pictures/Murray Cooper; 9 Shutterstock/kajornyot;
10 Shutterstock/David Havel; 11 Kingfisher Artbank; 11b Alamy/Bruce Farnsworth;
12–13 Kingfisher Artbank; 13 Shutterstock/Bildagentur Zoonar GmbH; 14 Shutterstock/Vadim
Petrakov; 15 Kingfisher Artbank; 15t Shutterstock/Dr Morley Read; 16–17 Shutterstock/Marcos
Amend; 18 Shutterstock/Ondrej Prosicky; 19b Shutterstock/Henrik Lehnerer; 19 Shutterstock/
aabeele; 20–21b Naturepl/Kim Taylor; 21t Shutterstock/Dmitry Kosterov; 22 Shutterstock/
Mikadun; 23 Shutterstock/macfuton; 24–25 Shutterstock/Colette3; 25t Shutterstock/
outdoorsman; 25b Shutterstck/Fruzsi-Gergo; 26 Shutterstock/Fikmik; 27t Shutterstock/
Michael Lynch; 27b Shutterstock/Noumae; 28–29 Shutterstock/Ja Ritnetikun; 29 Shutterstock/
ZONETEEn; 32 Shutterstock/Mikadun.
Cards: Front tl Shutterstock/Albie Venter; tr Shutterstock/Jiri Vaclavek; bl FLPA/Minden
Pictures/Michael & Patricia Fogden; br Shutterstock/Rich Carey; Back tl Shutterstock/
Destinyweddingstudio; tr Shutterstock/Bilal Shafi; bl Shutterstock/reptiles4all;
br Shutterstock/Mark Caunt.

Front cover: Red macaws rest on a branch.

CONTENTS

For your free audio download go to
http://panmacmillan.com/audio/
RemarkableRainforests **or** goo.gl/WjoDVO
Happy listening!

Fascinating rain forests

Rain forests are thick, lush forests with trees that stay green all year long. Most rain forests are tropical—they are found in some of the hottest places on Earth near the equator.

FACT ...

Misty rain forests called cloud forests grow high up on cool, damp mountain slopes.

The damp, warm climate is perfect for plants and wildlife. Rain forests are home to half of the plants and animals in the world.

The endangered mountain gorilla lives in the Congo rain forest.

SPOTLIGHT: The Congo

Famous for:	home of the mountain gorilla
Size:	580,000 sq. mi. (1.5 m sq. km)
Home to:	2000 types of animal
In danger from:	palm oil production

Lush layers

A tropical rain forest has four main layers. The emergent layer is the top of the tallest trees. The rain forest roof is called the canopy. Parrots, monkeys, and countless other animals live here.

Leafy bushes and the tops of small trees form the understory. The forest floor has little light and is filled with insects, ferns, and dead leaves.

The tiger is difficult to see in the shadows of the rain forest floor.

6

canopy layer

understory

forest floor

Life at the top

The tallest trees in the rain forest have their tops in the emergent layer. They feel the full force of the rain, the sun, and the wind.

The rare harpy eagle lives in the treetops of the Amazon rain forest.

The branches of the tallest trees can spread as wide as a football field. They are home to soaring eagles, noisy parrots, butterflies, bats, and monkeys.

Gibbons are the only apes to spend their entire lives up in the trees.

The noisy canopy

The busiest and noisiest part of the rain forest is the canopy layer. More animals live in the canopy than anywhere else in the rain forest.

The gray-headed lovebird is native to the island of Madagascar.

SPOTLIGHT: Madagascar

Famous for:	unique wildlife, including lemurs
Size:	1930 sq. mi. (5000 sq. km)
Home to:	thousands of unique animals
In danger from:	illegal logging

The canopy is home to monkeys, birds, snakes, and tree frogs. Many animals can leap or glide from one tree to another.

Howler monkeys leap from tree to tree.

FACT ...

Scientists build aerial walkways and fly in hot air balloons in order to study this hidden world.

The understory

The rain forest understory is humid and dark. The plants that grow here have large, dark-green leaves to catch the small amounts of light.

morpho butterfly

liana

yellow-banded poison dart frog

lobster claw plant

There is very little wind in the understory layer, so plants rely on insects and animals to pollinate their flowers. There are more insects here than anywhere else in the rain forest.

This panther chameleon likes the warm, wet conditions of the rain forest.

vine

tree frog

The forest floor

The forest floor is covered with dead leaves and twigs. These rot down and provide nutrients for the rain forest trees and plants. Tapirs and capybaras search for roots and tubers here, and it is home to small creatures such as millipedes, scorpions, spiders, and earthworms.

tree frog

Capybaras are related to guinea pigs.

FACT ...

Some of the largest tree trunks are 13 feet (four meters) across—that's as wide as two cars.

The blue-wing butterfly has a very long tongue to suck up nectar from flowers.

tapir

ants

poison dart frog

buttress root

15

The mighty Amazon

The biggest river in the world is the
Amazon. It gives its name to the
Amazon rain forest—the world's
largest tropical rain forest.

SPOTLIGHT: Amazon rain forest

Famous for:	the world's largest rain forest
Size:	2.1 m sq. mi. (5.5 m sq. km)
Home to:	millions of plants and animals
In danger from:	logging, farming, mining

The Amazon River is more than 4000 miles (6500 kilometers) long and is home to some amazing creatures, including piranhas, giant catfish, electric eels, river dolphins, manatees, caimans, snapping turtles, and capybaras.

The caiman is a fierce hunter.

Brilliant birds

More types of bird live in the tropical rain forest than anywhere else in the world. Rain forest birds can be all sizes and colors, from the tiny hummingbird to the enormous toucan.

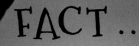

FACT...

Hummingbirds can beat their wings 12,000 times a minute. They are the only birds that can fly backward.

The toucan's huge beak helps
the bird stay cool.

Scarlet macaws have
sharp claws for climbing.

Insect armies

Thousands of tiny creatures such as beetles, ants, and woodlice scurry around the forest floor.

They feed on the rotting leaves and fungi. Many insects, such as ants and termites, live together in colonies that are organized like armies.

Leafcutter ants carry pieces of leaf back to their nest.

FACT...

Rain forest bugs have an important role: they break down the leaves that fall from above.

More than 50 different types of ant can live in an area of rain forest as small as five square feet (half a square meter).

King of the rain forest

The beautiful jaguar prowls along tree branches in the rain forest. Jaguars search the forest floor for mice or larger animals such as monkeys, tapirs, and deer.

Jaguars will even fight an alligator, and their powerful jaws can cut through a turtle's shell.

The jaguar moves very quietly on padded paws. Its spotted coat helps it blend into the rain forest shadows.

FACT ...

The jaguar is in danger of disappearing as its rain forest homes are destroyed.

The jaguar hunts monkeys like this squirrel monkey.

SPOTLIGHT: Jaguar

Lives:	Central and South America
Size:	about 5 ft. (1.5m) long
Eats:	most mammals
Conservation status:	threatened

Sssnakes

Snakes are some of the deadliest animals in a tropical rain forest. Many snakes catch frogs and other small animals on the forest floor and kill them with their venomous fangs. Other snakes squeeze their victims to death.

yellow anaconda

An emerald tree boa winds its body
around a branch and waits to catch its prey.

The giant
Madagascan
hognose snake
can grow
to 70 in.
(180cm) long.

Hairy and scary!

The Amazon rain forest is home to the largest spider in the world (the goliath tarantula) and the world's most venomous spider (the wandering spider).

Most tarantulas hunt for food rather than spin webs to trap it.

Vampire bats have very sharp teeth to bite into their prey without waking it up.

Around 1000 different types of bat live in the Amazon rainforest. They include the vampire bat, which bites into sleeping animals at night and then drinks their blood.

jumping spider

Rain forest future

Every second a piece of rain forest the size of a football field is destroyed to make a large farm, to extract minerals, or to build a road. This destroys the homes of countless animals and plants.

cleared rain forest

It also means there are fewer trees to take in carbon dioxide gas and give out the oxygen you breathe. Too much carbon dioxide in the air can cause global warming, which is when Earth heats up.

This periwinkle grows in the rain forests of Madagascar. It is used to make medicines that treat some types of cancer.

GLOSSARY

aerial walkway A rope bridge high up in the trees.

buttress A root that grows from a tree trunk and helps the tree stay upright.

canopy The "roof" of the rain forest, or its layer of high branches.

carbon dioxide A gas that is released into the atmosphere.

climate The general weather in an area.

colonies Groups of animals living together.

emergent layer The tallest trees in a rain forest, above the canopy.

fungi Living things that are not plants or animals, for example mushrooms and toadstools.

global warming A rise in temperatures on Earth.

mammal An animal that feeds its young with milk from its body.

minerals Valuable substances in rocks and soil.

nutrient Food that plants and animals need to take in so they can grow.

pollinate To transfer pollen from one flower to another, so that a new plant can grow.

prey Animals hunted for food.

tropical Describes warm places near the hottest part of the equator.

tuber The swollen stem of a plant, which grows underground.

understory The area above the forest floor where bushes and young trees grow close together.

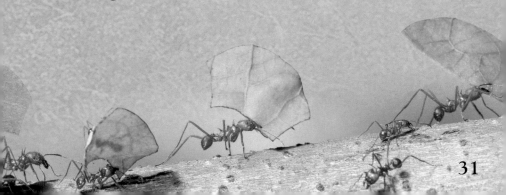

INDEX